Fun

Karen Durrie

MEDIA ENHANCED BOOKS

AV²
BY WEIGL™
ADDED VALUE • AUDIO VISUAL

Go to **www.av2books.com**, and enter this book's unique code.

BOOK CODE

J486418

AV² by Weigl brings you media enhanced books that support active learning.

AV² provides enriched content that supplements and complements this book. Weigl's AV² books strive to create inspired learning and engage young minds in a total learning experience.

Your AV² Media Enhanced books come alive with...

Audio
Listen to sections of the book read aloud.

Video
Watch informative video clips.

Embedded Weblinks
Gain additional information for research.

Try This!
Complete activities and hands-on experiments.

Key Words
Study vocabulary, and complete a matching word activity.

Quizzes
Test your knowledge.

Slide Show
View images and captions, and prepare a presentation.

... and much, much more!

Published by AV² by Weigl
350 5ᵗʰ Avenue, 59ᵗʰ Floor New York, NY 10118
Website: www.av2books.com   www.weigl.com

Library of Congress Cataloging-in-Publication Data

Durrie, Karen.
 Fun / Karen Durrie.
    p. cm. -- (Community helpers)
 ISBN 978-1-61690-944-4 (hardcover : alk. paper) -- ISBN 978-1-61690-595-8 (online)
 1. Community life--Juvenile literature. 2. Social participation--Juvenile literature. I. Title.
 HM761.D88 2012
 307.3'3--dc23
                              2011024903

Printed in the United States of America in North Mankato, Minnesota
1 2 3 4 5 6 7 8 9 0 15 14 13 12 11

062011
WEP030611

Project Coordinator: Karen Durrie Art Director: Terry Paulhus

Weigl acknowledges Getty Images as the primary image supplier for this title.

Fun

CONTENTS

Some workers
in our community
help us have fun.

Birdwatcher

Ride Operator

Clown

Gardener

Drum Teacher

Mountain Biking Teacher

Swimming Instructor

I show you how to ride a bike on hills, dirt, and rocks.

I am a mountain biking teacher.

I teach you how to plant seeds to grow food and flowers.

I am a gardener.

I make sure you are buckled in safely. I start and stop the rollercoaster.

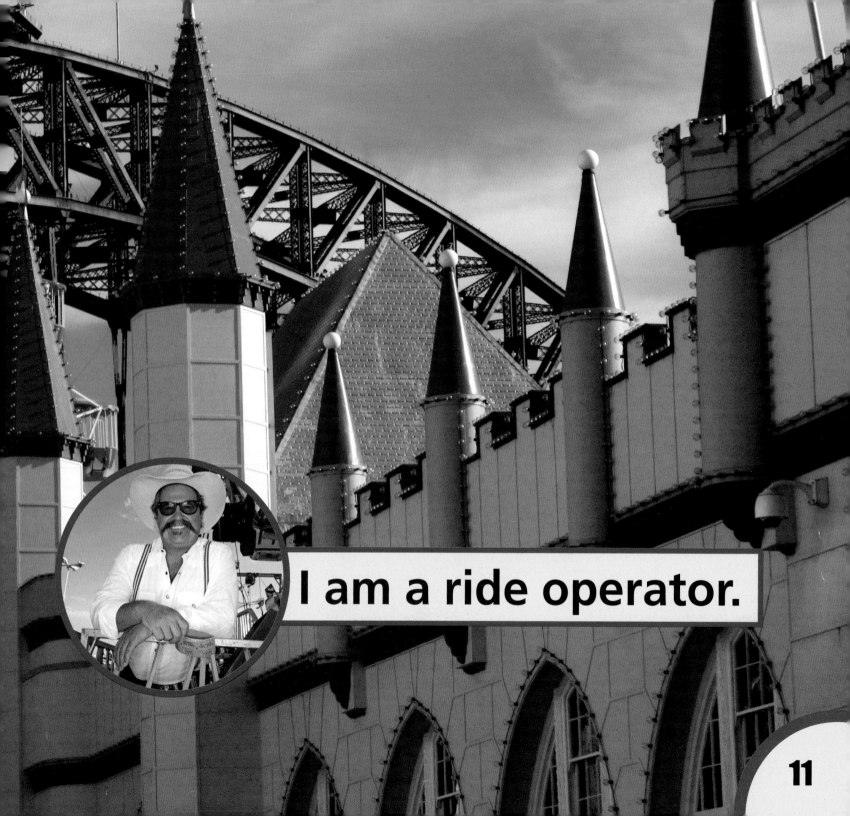

I am a ride operator.

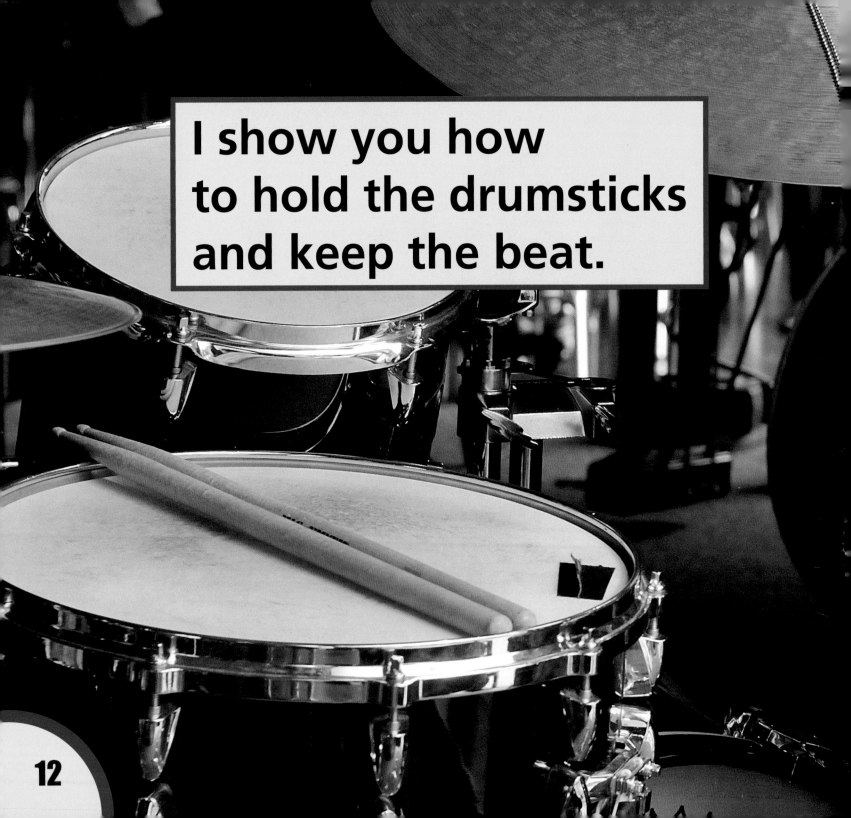

I show you how
to hold the drumsticks
and keep the beat.

12

I am a drum teacher.

I make you laugh at parties.

14

I am a clown.

I help you spot birds
and tell you about them.

I am a birdwatcher.

I teach you to float, kick, and swim in water.

I am
a swimming instructor.

I see people having fun in my community.

What do you do for fun?

FUN FACTS

People with common interests can form a community. Many jobs exist to help people have fun in their community. Having fun is an important part of being happy. Read more below about these helpers in our community.

Pages 4-5

Fun is a simple word for recreation. Recreation is an activity done purely for enjoyment. Recreational activities can be done together or alone and can include active and passive pursuits. Sports, gardening, hobbies, playing music, reading, and playing games are some types of recreation. There are many careers that focus on recreation.

Pages 6–7

Pathways and parks are built in many communities to encourage different kinds of recreation. Mountain biking is done on steep hills and rough terrain. It can be done in natural areas or at special parks where riders take lessons from skilled teachers. Many ski hills are used for mountain biking during summer months.

Pages 8–9

Gardening can be done at home or in a community garden. Some schools and neighborhood parks have community gardens. These places bring neighbors together to share a love of gardening. People may share the flowers or food the gardens produce.

Pages 10–11

Rides are found at fairs and amusement parks. People do many different jobs at amusement parks. Ride and game operators, mechanics, entertainers, food vendors, groundskeepers, and cleaners are some jobs at an amusement park.

WORD LIST

Research has shown that as much as 65 percent of all written material published in English is made up of 300 words. These 300 words cannot be taught using pictures or learned by sounding them out. They must be recognized by sight. This book contains 33 common sight words to help young readers improve their reading fluency and comprehension. This book also teaches young readers several important content words, such as proper nouns. These words are paired with pictures to aid in learning and improve understanding.

Page	Sight Words First Appearance
4	have, help, in, our, some
6	a, and, how, I, on, show, to, you
8	food, grow, plant
10	are, make, start, stop, the
12	keep
14	at
16	about, tell, them
18	water
20	my, people, see
21	do, for, what

Page	Content Words First Appearance
4	community, fun, workers
5	birdwatcher, clown, drum, gardener, instructor, mountain, operator, ride, teacher
6	bike, dirt, hills, rocks
8	flowers, seeds
10	rollercoaster
12	beat, drumsticks
14	parties
16	birds

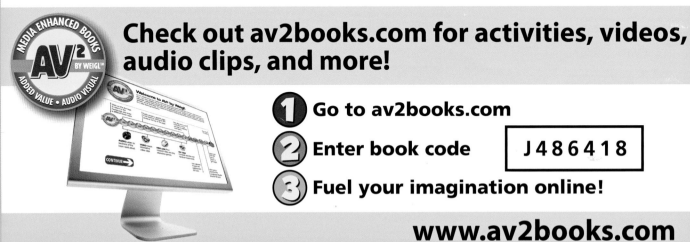
24